J. Müller

thank you for buying this book and supporting me. i am an independent singer, dj, producer, poet and creator of parth_é; a space to support you through your awakening. i have self-published 3 poetry books, "peaceful thoughts", "you are a mystic child"+ "medicine for a healing world". i have produced and released a host of tracks including my debut e.p, "j.müller 2.0" released in oct 2022 and i run a record label and conscious dance event called, "our sacred rhythms". through my brand parth_é, i am the host of "the new monks podcast", creator of the online course, 'awakening 101 - a ninja's guide to navigating your spiritual awakening', meditations and have expanded parth_é as a clothing brand. my purpose is to inspire the evolution of consciousness through art with all that i create.

listen to my music on spotify by taking a photo of the qr code below on your phone's camera.

www.jmuller.co
www.parthe.one

for the mystics, truth seekers and eternal beings.

if you have somehow found your way to these words, thank you for being here. i hope that they will inspire you more into remembering who you truly are and invoking peace along the way.

the greatest journey we can walk is the one that brings us into ourselves. farther. deeper.

may these words guide you into truth, love, light codes and sound tones for evolution.

it's time

this journey.
rollercoaster.
it has been 5 years since the start of my awakening
and plateau of peace is here.
i can finally say that the healing is healing now
but it's been healing that brought me here in the first place.
i live in the contradictions.
this year was a rapid one, slipstream time-hacking
just like the others.
the journey never ends.
growing infinitely closer to myself.
bringing back parts of me that went missing along the way.
traumatised. frozen.
broken. woken
up. healed. back
when spirit comes knocking for you to change your ways of being.
don't be afraid to answer the door
and walk through it.
although much a rapturous ride;
scary at times, confused, transient, discomfort in ways
i've never experienced before.
beauty in spades of magic i always believed
yet never saw.
best believe it's your time to answer the call.
and never will it arrive and you are not ready for.
ring ring.
hello?
it is time,
to wake up.

glow

you are a mystic child my love
few will understand your connection to the divine
but let that not cause you to deny it
and express it.
own your magic
and don't let their disagreements try tell you
what you already know to be true
because you can feel it,
more profoundly than any teaching ever told.
it's much deeper than thought
because it's what your soul already knows
and when you are homesick for the stars,
remember that it's pretty normal
for light to yearn to be amongst light.
for one day,
you will surely find your way home
and until then
glow.

this awakening is compulsory

you carried wounds within you
that weren't meant to be carried
for too long
and now the time has opened.
nature is healing
and the skies have opened
for you to heal too.
there is nowhere to hide
but inside
because
this awakening is compulsory
my friend.

we need people to feel

before you even start to open your mouth on the current state of affairs i would like to ask you these questions...

do you even know what it feels like to live with hundreds of years of oppression in your bloodline?

before you start to talk, have you even thought about what that would actually entail? to have inherited a sense of worthlessness and discrimination? we need to start feeling if we are going to start truly understanding and,

do you even know what it feels like to have had ancestors as slaves? imma say that again. do you even know what it feels like to have had ancestors as slaves? yes because that shit is real and it falls through generation to generation. it doesn't just disappear and now. we are living out the karma.

do you know what it feels like to have inherited that trauma? we need more empathy, understanding and compassion if we are to truly understand.

now it's a difficult one for sure because you can never really know how that feels. unless. you have hundreds of years of oppression in your bloodline. so before you start to speak. i ask you to seek these questions within yourself.

if i tell you that i am angry, can you see why? this broken unfamiliarly unfair system does not feel like home. and what. are you doing to try to understand and grow?

are you listening more clearly without your mind and with your heart? i mean do you even know. what that feels like for a start? babe it's a freaking mess. i'll tell you that for free. but what about our freedom?

do you know what it would have felt like to fight for equality during the apartheid? or the black panthers or the slave trade or the cops when they stop you for no reason at all? i mean. there are many more examples...

can you see why that fight is still within us? because we inherited oppression and it still lives on amongst us and babe do you even know what it feels like to be born into this madness?

that was somebody else's problem in the first place and now it is my own.

i didn't ask for the colour of my skin. nobody did. yet here we all are.

do you know what it feels like to be black in 2020 as your history lives on?

now before you start talking. i want you to ask yourself some questions and i want you to take your time with them and please. i want to feel your empathy in the words that you speak so that i know your compassion is real.

because right now. more than ever. *we need people to feel.*

this is not our only problem. but through them all. we can start looking a little deeper in order for us all. to heal.

welcome. to the great awakening family. now what are you going to do. to heal?

the gods of the ocean

the gods of the ocean know the waves, that will direct you on your way
home.

where every feeling is valid, every encounter important.

they won't tell you directly how but they are constantly guiding you through instinct and will continue to do so until you listen.

the real flow is in not seeing the flow. people will tell you to stop fighting, to stop resisting and accept what is but the truth my dear is that everything is and the 'fighting' is also part of that flow. it all is.

there are no rules, you create the rules but it will ask a lot from you to listen to the whispers of the waves that wash ever so silently, following their direction through your days.

through everything you go through in life, they just want you to experience your expansiveness.

when you follow the whispers of the gods all the way through, via the people you meet in your life and the events that occur. there is no need for protection from the hurt, for you already are protected.

sometimes you think you need to protect yourself but that protection is just for your ego and your small self. and when you travel through the 'hurt', when you realise that it's not painful to you but only to your ego, *that's when you find your way home.*

and it is a much more powerful feeling than setting your standards, and not accepting less than you deserve, judging someone else's actions and your own, feeling disrespected or hard done by because when there is no hurt, there is only experience. it is truth and it overrides all else.

more than you can ever know, the gods wish to delight in your embodiment of their kind of protection. and that protection is called *unconditional love.*

the ocean wishes to embrace you in it
if you can seek below your limits.

    deeper.
    and trust.

rising

my forbidden fruit.
the divine sacred feminine.
the one that we were all taught not to embrace.
for her power is unparalleled in this universal space.
well, guess what babes?
she be rising.
through centuries and centuries we denied her throne
and her power was lost to the meek and unknown.
but guess what babes?
she be rising.
because we were so afraid of her majestic reign,
we constantly consistently denied her name.
but she.
is remembering.
that the power
is always,
has always
been hers.
yet the question that is left,
still remains,
can you step up and match up to her game?
because i'll tell you one
things
are not going to stay the same.
for we.
are rising.

only the brave tread the path of truth

what if i told you that your destiny is to become lighter
let go of the baggage,
transcend the heaviness?
would you know how to release?
would you even try and see?
what if i told you that you have one purpose in this life
and that is to open the flow of energy in your being?
would you believe me?
and what if i said that the most important thing
that you can do
is to work on releasing
all. that. stuff.
that you've been carrying around for years, centuries,
lifetimes.
and this precious human life
is the only tool for you to do that...
what if i told you that all you have to do
is to figure out how,
to become lighter
and that was it,
would you even bother?

to be cleansed by the rain

this one is for you. walking through the storm. watching everything fall. removing the layers of noise and nonsense. everything that isn't you. everything that doesn't serve you. everything that doesn't belong to you. everything that causes pain. everything that is not peace. everything that is not in service of your highest good. watching it all crumble so that you can find out who you truly are. and why you are here. so that you can make sense of the madness. well done for continuing to walk in the rain. to be cleansed by the source and heal from your pain. well done for being so courageous again and again and again.

nature's calling

she whispers to you throughout the day,
the light is calling from beyond the haze.
a full spectrum of energies, darkness to light,
colours, sounds, opinions, vibrations, shades.
but tell me,
what are you tuning into babe?

conversations with my inner child. II

tell me about your pain
i wanna hear your story
it deserves to be told
in compassionate loving glory.
i'm here only to listen
so you can voice your position
and finally
we can let go of inner wounds
of being silenced in childhood
+ other truths
and imma be loving you completely fully boo.

stay soft my love

if you can stay soft
in a world that teaches us not to,
that promotes reaction over action.
if you can stay soft
after so many people disrespecting you.
if you can hold love and compassion within your heart
through it all.
if you can understand the truth that those who inflict pain
are also in pain:
you are powerful. this is real strength,

to be vulnerable is a superpower
not many people have the courage to show.

she lives for the healing

she lives for the healing
and she will die for the freedom.
for that seed is planted within us
from the very day that we are born.
she is the sorcerer of her own
kind of magic.
you know,
the kind that is infectious
because it undeniably affects us.
she knows that we are ever free,
only just a little bit blinded
by our own spiritual amnesia, we,
somehow forgot.
and she is on a mission.
you know,
the one where we all remember
who we truly are
and unite in peace.
unbounded,
we will meet in that place
and dance the dance
that is forever
in our hearts.
see you there amigos!

spirituality = practicality, trust

i'm not really interested in your intellectual theories tbh.
i'll be interested in you if you can listen
more than you speak.
be non-judgemental even if you disagree.
if you can look me in the eye without any awkwardness
and ask more questions than trying to give me answers to
things i haven't even asked for.
do you enjoy the silences between our words?
and can you pay close attention to me,
when i am speaking,
am i heard?
how present are you in our conversation?
can you be humble and admit your flaws?
including the fact that there is so much more to what we
know for sure?
are you uncertain because you know of this too?

i don't care about your beliefs.
i want to know if you can laugh with me through the grief
and pain and be silly as well as serious in this game.
these are my foundations and in reality,
spirituality = practicality.
trust me, you don't have to tell me how deep you are into
your mystical journey because
i already know
just from the ways in which your actions have shown.

i am a work in progress

sometimes we forget
that we can have multiple things at once.
maybe because we don't think that we deserve it
or because we think that we have to get to a certain place
before we can welcome something
else into our lives.
but i just want to let you know
that you deserve everything that you wish for
and you are allowed to accept it –
even though, you are a *work in progress*.
because things *can* work
better
when together.

nothing's really ever as it seems

i lost myself
and found myself
completely outside of what i used to know, used to like, used to be.
and that's when i found a whole new field of discovery.
because the labels that used to define me
didn't matter anymore
as i found my flexibility.
i swear i'm the biggest hypocrite in the two thousand and teens
because honestly,
i don't even recognise me.

show me your values

what does it mean to do the right thing?
because it takes a little courage to voice your opinions
but it takes a *whole lot more*
for your beliefs to become you in *action*.
i want to see your values in the details of your life
where it matters the most.
i want to see if you can make the moral decision
in silence,
when no-one is watching?
i want to know if honesty, virtue and integrity
are important to you?
can you embody these,
in *everything*
and *no matter*
what
you do?

$free.99

the wonderment is free.
the all encompassing love, is free.
the truth is free.
autonomy is free.
connection is free.
only if you dare
to enter the temple
of the unknown.
will you go?

as long as you feel it

feeling my way through
healing my heart through feeling.

more together

but can you feel the connection?
you know, the one where i am connected to you and you are connected to me
and together we coincide in peace?
truth is, if you can't feel it,
then there shall be no peace
but just the illusion of a partition
between each other
truth is, we are not separate
but it's up to you what you choose to tune into.
there is a place that exists where
no judgements persist.
where understanding underlies
all of our interactions in this life.
where support is unbounded with
acceptance through the waters of change.
yes, this place exists.
are you ready to meet me there?
because i feel the connection,
you know, the one where i am connected to you and you are connected to me
and i think that together we can coincide in peace.
i want to be there for you,
because this is all that i know to be real.
and life, can be hard on us at times
or maybe that's just our perception of it
but it still feels like a hard tumbling of bricks.
heavy.
but it's o.k because together
we can conquer all.
we were born connected and forever we shall be
it's easy to forget because we can't see
but remember,
i will always be here in the depths of your heart
to remind you,
that i've always been with you from the start.

interconnected

we were taught the law of separation.
the world divides us, as can be seen from the invisible
barriers between countries.
but that's exactly what they are; invisible.
we are taught to hold onto the pride of provenance but
what about the pride of humanity
or the pride of nature?
in which all things spring from...
what about the law of interconnectivity?
why limit our association to exclude parts of humanity?
when the grandest truth is one of unity.
only that we merely believe in separation
and we leave others behind
with the divisions held within our societies
and within
our own minds.

get free

free yourself of everything
but the imagination.

i came here to move mountains

you don't see what i'm doing
because you live the illusion
but
i came here to move mountains.

it's a longer path
but instant gratification is not my graft
because
i came here to move mountains.

and one day you'll see
from the endeavour of consistency
how
i came here to move mountains.

it's time to close the door

it's time to close the door
that was left ajar for far too long.
it's time to close the door
because i don't want to play this complex song.
i don't want to dance anymore
because it's become quite suffocating,
inconsistent, and always unsure.
words without actions just remaining in thoughts
it's time to close the door
and really all i want to do right now
is fly.
just the same way
that i flew before.

everything is perfect

get present. practice awareness of self. remember that everything happens on time. and what's happening right now, is perfect. every single day. remember. meditate. stay present. practice nurturing self-awareness. forget. and then remember, that there is nothing to worry about. because everything is right. right now. *everything is perfect.*

notes on self-love

you already know how beautiful you are.
you are already complete, dear one.
and in those moments when you forget,
you just need to
remember.
a part of the divine creation;
you already are all of the affection that you need.

back to basics

less
external validations,
more
self-love.

are you ready for your rebirth?

this is the path that we tread slowly,
lightly and meaningfully.
to break the cycle that has travelled
the ancestral lines.
to bring the darkness into view
in order to turn it into light.
to be the alchemists
because we are the magicians too.
to usher in a new state of being
amongst an ancient way of living.
because we know that it exists.
right here, right now.
and this is where the journey begins.
it is time.
are you ready for your rebirth?
because it is coming,
whether you like it or not.

boundless and

i get very claustrophobic with
the labels
you try to put on me
because
i know who i am —

free.

being truthful

let's allow each other to be
and get to know one another
truthfully.

the waiting room

this week i jumped from depths of sorrow
and felt it through and through.
i then turned it on its head to gratitude.
through thoughts of worry, to thoughts of peace.
in an instance.
and i wondered how can these opposites be
so close together in such a short distance?
in all honesty,
i didn't know which one to feel,
which one was real?
maybe this is just the deal —
they're both here living happily together.
so i neither held on or let go to either
and i then found myself
in the waiting room.
untethered.

just as i should be

i'm sorry that you can't hold me in
all of my glory
and you feel the need to change a
divine goddess' story.
but the angels are lost in a perpetual
wonder you see
and you will never succeed
becuase i am,
just
as i should be.

soul family

raw. open. vulnerable. unfiltered.
expression of each other to each other.
unafraid to be seen.
floating through our streams
of consciousness.
i guess we coincided with trust
and bumped into wanderlust.
amongst the glistening light of the stars
lies the universe in the dark.
as opposites coinciding together,
as if being apart from one another,
never.
we don't know where their journey began,
yet here they are.
all i know is that i feel like we met in a
foreign land,
yet here we are.
present.
yet
familiar.

searching but not searching

searching for that place
where i keep searching for that place
of overthinking
near that place of worrying about the outcome,
which is right next to that feeling of fear
but really i'm searching
for that place of clarity.
right next to that place of peace,
which is right by that place of presence,
next door to the place of acceptance
and the place of trust,
which is actually a place
where i'm not searching.

are. you. ready?

imma take you on a journey
where you forget everything you've learnt
but tell me first –
are you ready to let it all go
and do the search?
the truth waits only for those
who comprehend it's worth.

for the subtle queens

i am a subtle queen.
and i don't feel the need
to shout and scream.

there are enough people
shouting and screaming.

make way for the empaths.
we're coming through,
stat.

i just want to play

please take down the imaginary wall
that you created between us
and then we can play.

less equals more

less
chasing thoughts,
more
presence.

flow: a feeling of serene tranquility within the cells of your body no matter the outside circumstances.

i've been thinking a lot about the idea that sometimes we resist the 'flow' of life and we should just 'let it go' but to me everything is designed for our experience and there is an importance in the resisting. as it is also part of the flow of life. i believe that the real flow is actually a *state of being*. no matter what is happening in your life or whether you are 'holding on' or not. you can still be *in the flow*.

we need more of you

to all the goddesses out here.
the ultimate creators.
the witches.
the mystics.
the healers.
the feelers.
the vulnerable emotional revealers.
the female boss's.
the ones now and before us
who have had to stand up under this patriarch.
we are the mothers and the daughters.
the very reason of existence.
for we carry the seed to create – life.
and we wouldn't be here without it.
now that is real power and magic.
please don't forget that you are born with it.
rise feminine.
rise.
wild woman,
rise.
and run,
run wild into the world spreading it
the world needs more of...
you.

only few dare to tread the path

i keep going further and further
into the depths of infinity
and the more i travel,
the less you will understand of me.
but that is just the price of ascension,
a slight space in comprehension.

are you with us?

lately i've been thinking about how i'm making an impact to see the world the way that i envision it because you know, if i think about the future. or let's start now. if i think about right now. there are so many backwards ways of being, of thinking, of teaching. wild things are gwarning that don't even make sense. that are not for us and by us, i mean the human race. weird invisible divisions between people and within ourselves that stop us from being our actual selves. to me, it no comprendre and then i think about the future and i think, are we really going to keep playing this game? you know the one where we suffer and are in pain and are blinded so much that we can't even see what's beneath our own names. and the ones with the torch shine the light to show the way but there's always going to be the ones who are stuck in their darkness stepping on toes along the way. so we do this dance like this and it just keeps going round and round and maybe that's just it. perhaps. but i see a different future for us and by us, i mean the human race. i see harmony and i would like you to see harmony too. the future is as we create it so i ask you to create it too. join the dance of liberation, the only one dance of our souls emancipation. we were born to be free and forever we shall seek this journey until we find our way home. if you're with us there's no waiting more. let's co-create the future that we are all waiting for...

reveal yourself

being yourself is nothing short of
revolutionary
and i'm talking about the you
that perhaps
you don't even know,
yet.

feminine energy

oh how i yearn to be
wild, feminine and free.

no restrictions zone

yeah that's right.
keep walking unless you can hold me
in all of my power, glory and magic.

levels

i found confidence that you wouldn't believe.
it's got nothing on insecurity,
trust me.

floating on a cloud

and one day you will be floating on a cloud of unlimited amazingness asking yourself; how did i get here? then you will know that all of the darkness and pain was never really darkness and pain anyway. it was all just directions on the path of life. steering you to becoming a more whole, complete and truer being than you've ever been and experiencing life from a much lighter, joyful and grateful experience. this is it. we are here. in time and space. experiencing life by breathing through it day and night. not knowing what the future brings. and you will know that no matter how much pain and suffering you had to go through to get here. it was all worth it, in the end. because now we are free. and some days you may sink back to that place but it won't matter because now you know that it is all designed for you, not against you and you will embrace it, remembering that this place exists. and know that it is unlimited. floating on a cloud.

in flow

i want to let life take me
wherever it wants to go.
forever
in flow.

do what i do

i do what i do
because there is no other path when
you're tuned into the frequency of your heart.
intuition guides my every move
and *i trust*.

that's what i call alchemy

the future can be different from the past.
the future can be different from the past.
the future can be different from the past.

she shines

now is the time
for the divine feminine
to shine.

the whispers

babe, just fall.
we will catch you
with unbounded support.
believe in what you already know to be true
because we got you.

far beyond it

life lives within the present.
beyond the notions of time.

my intuition is telling me there'll be better days

the only right decision
is to follow your intuition.

be a kind person

all that you have to do is be a kind person. be honest with everyone that you deal with. be gentle, be considerate. be a human with feelings and if you can't do that, *find the ways how.* find your values that will always show you how. don't allow your baggage to get in the way of your relationships with others. don't play games with people. you're only messing with the *energies of the universe*, which will *always* come back to bite you one day. be a real human being. you deserve that. we all do.

i dedicate this one to you

i dedicate this one to you. you've come a long way and yet there is still so far to go. you are the reason for where you are right now. keep pushing through your own magic. all that matters is that you are being your most authentic self in all the ways that you know how to. everything else is secondary. and if you've not quite made it to the expression of who you are. know that you will find the ways to push past your own barriers and conditioning. those voices that tell you not to. those ones who warn you to get back onto the road when you're clearly more than half way down the road less travelled and it is all for good reason. and they will see, one day, it will make sense. you can have what you want in this life, with an infinite amount of trust, otherly guidance and heightened awareness that you're tuned into. it's a powerful force that only once you know, you will know. and you know, that everything is happening exactly just the way that it was planned. may you embody infinite trust in your capability to create what you were brought onto this planet to create and infinite trust that the universe will bring it all in divine timing. because it will. as long as you are expressing your authenticity now. *that is the only way how.*

to clear the haze

surrender to your feelings
because they always show you the way.
let your intuition guide you
and help to clear the haze.

inscending to ascend

have you been to the depths of your imagination?
do you know what resides there?
have you dared to go down that rabbit hole?
and let go of what you know?
can you let the magic of this mystery take control over your body/mind and guide you to the palace of eternity?
how much can you actually let go?
because there is a world waiting to be explored beyond the depths of what is known,
tangible, historical.
and it's hidden deep within the depths of imagine nation
my love, it is mystical.
and you will be reborn.
into a more powerful, more truthful, more authentic version of you.
more connected to your senses of *feeling*
and it merely depends on your willingness
to push the restart button
on everything
again and again and again and –
inscending to ascend.

calling all my peoples

remember that you don't have to bend yourself
in order to fit into someone else's perception of the world.
the ones who understand you
will never ask you to bend.
the ones who understand you
will accept you to no end.
don't be fooled by conditional love –
that is only dealt by those who don't know that
anything better exists.
keep searching.
keep waiting.
there's no need to settle
because one day
you will find
your soul tribe.

the biggest deceit ever

i think that one of the most dangerous
things we were taught,
is to avoid and resist pain.

integrity so truth

she had an integrity so pure
that she could look you
dead in the eye and say,
"babe it's o.k,
you can trust me."
and know
that it was the truth.

super calm peace state

through time
you will find
that i'm more sensitive than shy.
yet stronger than what meets the eye.
i'm not 'emotional'
just feeling it all
and then
letting it fall
through the small act
of not being attached.

only you can save yourself

trauma fills my history
but the future is screaming liberty
because
of healing in the present.

power is hidden within your sensitivity

babe,
you are strong enough now
to become *gentle*.

i wonder why we constantly strive to change things outside of ourselves?

this world can be so harsh.
unknowingly,
we project.
please remember that
if anyone tries to make you feel as if
you are a probem.
the problem is not you.
more often than not,
it never is.
you are perfect.
i wonder why
we constantly strive
to change things
outside of ourselves.

come home babe. you are safe here

it is time to delete
your automatic stress response.
it is no longer needed
and you are safe here.

don't know about stalling

life never hurts.
the love never learns
and i just keep on falling.
don't know about stalling
to you.
do you
believe?
all you have to do is stop.
stand outside of yourself and drop.
everything
that you believe.
do you trust me?

just you and i

you know that magic place that transports you into another space. yeah, this is mine. and i'll have you, if you'll have me. and i'm ready to get lost in you__forever__just you and i.

come closer impermanence, i see you

sometimes what you thought was the destination was actually just a tunnel to go through__not to go to. because we can't see into the distance. until we get closer to it. and we will never know. until we *take that risk.*

careful or you'll get burnt

i am fire
because i walked through it
and came out the other side
more than a woman
vibrating
higher.

full spectrum

imagine.
if we could see
all
of
the colours.

spread your wings

spread your wings
into
the infinity
of your expansion.

learning those natural laws of the universe

slowly. and naturally.
everything falls exactly where it is supposed to be.
no need to interfere with it.
and try and correct the course of it.
just follow that intuition
and you will find.
the magic of flow.
that everything.
always balances out.
in the end.

imagine

imagine what we could create
if we all believed
in magic...

warrior of courage / stream of consciousness

what is this thing that we call life? how did we end up here? and what exactly are we doing here? i mean these philosophical questions have been asked throughout millennia but really. this year with this pandemic has been an absolute game. changer. time to really think about what's happening close to home and much deeper than that. like, why are we here without any recollection of how we got here? what is that about? and yes i've heard some theories. which, could be true. but like, how come we don't know? and don't know anybody who knows you know, do you?

and what is this cycle, with the battle between darkness and light? that just continues to go round in circles. and if i want to help others in some way. help the human race. what is the best way that i can do that, in order to not perpetuate this cycle? get lost in the illusion. how do we shatter the illusion? and not try to get others to jump on our bandwagon like, "i found the truth! it's this way!" because i really think that the truth is everywhere to be seen. the fibres of life are hidden in plain sight. and we just keep going round and round and round. until we stop. to notice. to feel. slow down. to listen a little more deeply. there are so many paths. it can be overwhelming deciding which one to choose. but the right path is the one that you choose. always.

and we keep searching and searching. but. what are we searching for? will we know once we find it? does this questioning ever end? are we regaining our memory? of magic and wizardry? once your mind opens completely. you begin to realise that everything is a possibility. and it is true. depending on your perspective. depending on what you can see. but when you blow the doors of perception open fully. magic and wizardry are an obvious possibility. of course they are real. and why should we limit ourselves to the smallest crumbs in believing it's not true?

honestly, do you know why we're here? and within this chaos and noise of 'haveago' shamans and false prophets, false light and all the like. how do you find your centre? when your whole world is crumbling apart? maybe that is the most important part of it all. i mean, does it really matter what path you choose, if they are all heading in the same direction? and to know that is to feel true equanimity. then it doesn't matter what happens along the way. it's all just to be experienced. but what if that is just a thought to have you complacent and not recognise what to do? how to act? what if, in fact there is a specific route that takes us to the emerald city? we question everything still.

and amongst the noise of right and wrong and people telling you what to do, what not to do and how to live your life. literally, go into any book store and you can see that it's full of books telling us what to do. but we're called human beings not human doings and. where did we get so accustomed to seeking everything outside of ourselves? it's embedded in our culture.

when do we get to the point where we start reclaiming our sovereignty. and remembering? remembering our magic and wizardry and why we are here? can you find that sweet spot? the one that screams neutrality? the one that doesn't get lost in what's right or what's wrong? perceives it all and accepts it all? and takes accountability? there is no right and wrong. then why does it feel like it? this duality of this human experience. getting lost in addictions. the craving. the craving. isn't it so hard to just sit still? and not allow someone to knock you off your centre?

and that will be your biggest task my friend. because even as you find your centre. trust, someone around the corner will be there to shake you. it's all just a test. to test your *autonomy*.

and the darkness and belief that this world is bad, is it just an illusion? because once you start focusing on creating love you can kind of forget about it. but the darkness can consume you into fear. gets kind of confusing but still we'll keep asking until the questions keep coming. and maybe they'll become clear? and we can find ourselves closer to truth? and the darkness is nothing to be afraid of no matter who, why, what it is. as long as you are vibrating in love, acceptance and truth. there is literally. *nothing. to be afraid of.*

and does this journey of healing ever end? they say it lasts a lifetime my friend. it's a paradox. the gurus. the wise ones. they tell us to look within. but. we have to find them without in the first place in order for us to look within. but. maybe we never had to look for them outside of ourselves in the first place? it's all just a game to get utterly lost in. the ultimate cosmic joke.

and who created it? perhaps it was i because i am creating it now. understanding infinity is completely mind expanding. but don't you forget to have fun along the way. breathe. because all this magic is you. and that can be a lot to comprehend.

and so we march backwards into the future. trusting the call within our spirit. careful not to tune into the darkness of the matrix and perpetuate it. but from the deepest parts of your soul, you trust. you trust the voice that tells you which way to go.

because there is nothing else to do. they say that all paths lead to our one home. and there is no right or wrong. and even though the criticism will surely come. from the people who love to point fingers all over the place. you trust yourself. because what else is there to do?

and so you walk.

one foot in front of the other.
content in your search.
trusting the mystery.
courageously
into the unknown.

sailing the seven seas

the thing about sailing the seven seas
is that one's navigation is key
not really to know your destination
but to flow with the waves and stand centred,
simply.

how are you living?

we've still got to do our best regardless of what other people are doing and regardless of what we see in our worldview. *it's a brave new kind of world* emerging this decade. how are you living? are you doing the things that you believe in? are you taking the steps to create the world that you believe in? are you cultivating a special kind of care and respect for our planet and it's inhabitants? are you expanding your mind and heart to feel these things and *more?*

are you overcoming your fear and anxiety that we are programmed with? can you even be yourself? do you even know what that looks like, feels like? do you even know who you are? are you even asking yourself these questions? and more importantly, are you doing something about it? or will you get stuck in fear? what else are you *doing* that is more important than your own evolution?

the revolution starts now and the protest can be felt deep within. it is time for change my friend.

always stay in touch

the mystery of the magic and the wonder and
the magic of the wonder and the mystery and
the wonder of the mystery and the magic.
always stay in touch.

yours truly

you are free
to discover your truth.

right in the centre of it all

connected to earth and ether
you know what it feels like
in the centre?
that's where you'll find me
and maybe you can meet me here,
where the magic persists
and the mystery consists
of dichotomies?
easy.

lightly mi amor

what happens when
everything becomes so meaningful
that it becomes meaningless?
perhaps there is no difference between the two.
in disguise the emptiness arrives
through moments of depth,
when you get used to depth
and intertwined between the lines
there appears to be no difference between
what's meaningful
and what's meaningless.

i wonder

every now and then
i revel in the mystery of life
and every now and then
i wonder why
things happen
the way that they happen
when they happen
in space and time.

and still

feeling powerful
as the tower falls
life out of your hands
and still
within it.

it's all you baby

when your response is different
people respond *differently*.

surrender to high power

what a relief it is to surrender
and to know and to feel and believe
that you got me.

swim good babe

i have depths
as deep as the ocean
that can only be known
when
you swim
below
the surface.

preparing for the elements

if you bring the fire
we'll bring the wind.
show me what you feel beneath your skin.
we've got the earth
solidly ting
but the fluids, the water my love,
we may need to swim!

no more labels. are you in?

oh what it means to be a woman. in a world that was not designed for us to feel equal. and what it means to be a man, in a world that was not designed for them to feel feminine at all. oh what it means to fit in-between and not have a label to attribute to. *identity crisis*. what does it mean to be a human? in a world that is in pain. suffering from centuries of grief and disdain? but i feel you. the prized position of standing in your authenticity but. some people won't like that. good luck when most of our programming teaches us the complete opposite of freedom. it's just you against the world. because no matter what. there will always be those with unsolicited opinions. that never ends. and you have to keep choosing yourself. again and again and again. but eventually you stop listening and being affected by the voices and you listen more closely to yourself instead. yet, it can still be a constant conflict stepping into your individuality. <u>it's your power</u>. *and this is the price of freedom.* are you in?

find it

there are moments when life forces you to slow down. *this is one of them*. and when everything slows down, it's easier to see the leaves more clearly when they land. embrace the time. there is a light. that is shining on everything right now. find it. because within it. you will be able to see more clearly. and when you can see more clearly. things start to change. *you* start to change. a new world is just a change of perspective away. and that new world is now. the light is bringing our outdated ideas and ways of being under scrutiny and i'm not talking about the people in power. i'm talking about you and i. and we have a choice: continue living the same way after everything blows over. or wake. the fxck up. and face yourself for sure. now it's up to you babe. but i'll tell you one thing — nature never really cared that death. is just. around. the corner.

stay protected amigos

all the feelings that we feel
never mind, 'are they even real?'
are they even ours
to *feel?*
yes, stay protected
in your boun-da-ries.

she is guiding the way

there is an opportunity that is arising through all of the noise. wait. stop. listen. focus. pay attention. what is really happening here? it's time to feel and it's time to start tuning in to reality. it is time to start waking up to our very own mysticism. because we are human beings waking up to our multidimensional beingness. listen more and talk less. it's time to feel because that is how we heal. the answers lie within. uncertainty is certainly certain. it always was. but it's o.k. all you have to do is surrender and trust. and the time is now. there are major shifts happening right now for all of us because we have been living in a very outdated way of being for too long now. and it is being exposed. observe as the tower falls because there is an opportunity that is arising through all of the noise. but the choice is ours. trust it is time for change. and mother earth knows this. for she. is guiding the way...

one fine line

one fine line of communication
between me and the divine.
its time to tune in more attentively
as the words start to flow abundantly.
the time is now.
the place is here.
as we move into a new stratosphere.
and the message received is loud and clear:
it's time for the birth of a new era my dear
and the fall of the system
and it's fear.
but enjoy the ride
as a new cycle is birthed
amongst the nation.
and you are a participant
within it's creation.

go

when your intuition is so strong
and you know you're on your soul path.
no matter what anybody says
it will never be able to
stop you.

baby i've been calling

wait, can you hear that? the world is calling you with wild abandon. if you listen carefully. it's in the leaves of the trees as the wind blows through them. it's in the sun as it rises and sets beyond the horizon. and the darkness of the sky at night. it's in the water in the ocean, in your shower every morning and the glass that you drink every day. if you listen carefully to the sounds of the cosmos. it's in every single detail of your life. it's within and without, lighting the way. for you to walk forwards. but tell me, *are you listening babe?*

it's your life baby

it's your life baby. live within your own rules. reclaim your authority. seek all from within. remember who you are. know that. and so much more. believe in yourself. no matter what. this life is made for dreams. dream them into being. be wary of all things of false light nature. learn how to use your discernment with your intuition. deepen your discernment so that you can avoid all of the traps. or maybe just some of them. there are many. but you will be infinitely protected as long as you keep believing in yourself and your ability to follow your own choices.

trust yourself. and find your connection to source. dance with it. this is your life. there's no need to follow trends. just be you. live life on your own terms. whatever direction you flow in. find your point of neutrality so that you can walk in and out of the fire with calm. it can get crazy. but if you have a strong foundation, nothing can touch you. everything is a lesson. be grateful for it all. because this is your life. i don't care who tries to tell you how to live your life. do not believe them or follow their lead – if it makes zero sense for you. many figures of authority are corrupted. no need to follow them.

follow the path of purity and truth. i mean, this will always be your choice. you always have a choice. don't believe anyone who tells you otherwise. especially yourself. but what's the point in living unless you are in integrity with the organic. with yourself. with all that is of divine nature. absolute power corrupts absolutely. follow what's true, real and feels right. and trust that you will know it when you need to. calm. life doesn't need to be lived in fight or flight mode. we can move past that zone. already. be free my love.

station create

when you create
and you start to see the potential
that you *can create*.
it's everything.
because
it is infinite.
and that's when you
start to get in touch with
the infinite.

more home than home

she never found a home in her hometown
that's why she's leaving
imagine
so long feeling out of place
always misplaced
that's why she's dreaming
of other lands
where the love flows deeper
and she
can plant her feet home in the sand.

it is your choice

we are just a product of our thoughts
so the question is...
what is inside your mind?
how do you transcend the limiting thoughts and beliefs
that have been programmed?
how do you get through
to your true essence?
how do you feel your emotions
and not let them determine your actions?
and ultimately,
choose the life that you want to live
and choose your reality?
rather than let it choose you?
how do you choose love?

the great purge

new body
new dreams.
close encounters
with everything.

find the others

there aren't many like you
you know
who mean what they say
and say what they mean and
are honest to a point of integrity
and it'll be even harder
to find the others.

forever we play

when you stop being triggered
by what people say
then you have all of the
freedom to play.

than anything else

and then you start to realise
that your peace is
so much more important
than anything else.

welcome to 12d

full power
energy transmissions
anytime.
anywhere.
welcome to 12d.

embodied

it's not about thinking
or believing
it's about being
and trust me
there's a different.

looking for all the other dreamers

dreaming dreams
of dreamers dreaming.
coming through to get you boo.

in gratitude and service to my purpose and plan

i am the vessel.
and in trust.
i move.
divinely supported
and playing out precisely
as it should be.
ain't no time like the present.
thank you for the clarity
in guidance on the path.
i see trust.
i speak trust.
and i feel trust.
let's *move*.

just tune in

it's around you.
all that you seek.
is within your grasp.
but it comes not with hesitation.
not with cowardice.
not with impatience.
not with the ego.
and not with power.
my lover,
it comes with humbly bowing to a far greater power.
and knowing that exists within you.
and more importantly feeling that within you.
and being the channel for it to express itself.
my love.
this has got *absolutely nothing*.
to do with you.
yet you.
are the channel.
just tune in.

clarity + growth

because amazingness is all around us
in every colour and
expression of who we are.
always forwards never backwards.
we see to the stars.

in your power

and one day
it will come back to you
without it for so long
you almost forgot
what it means
to stand in your power
but the only thing
left to do
is to *stand*.
in your power.

here with you

fall with me
into the other realms
where we'll lose track of time.
a year passing in a week
things are never as they seem
but i promise
i'll always be beside you
in your dreams.

we float like air

because we have let go of *everything*
not because we don't care.
we float like air.

exorcising insecurity

exorcising insecurity
to be felt again
back to your earliest memories
of when
you felt you weren't enough.
something of lacking
not receiving attention
a distant memory from a child's
perspective.
and as adults an abuse.
gaslighting and turning onto you.
we are exorcising insecurity
to be felt again.
this time to pull up a pew
come through
to a different kind of view.
when did it start?
i ask.
from the passing on of a parents
neglecting
inheritance in heritage.
and do we just pass it on?
or do we stand bold and walk toward
secure connections?
change the narrative through
different actions
truth is.
i don't ever remember feeling secure
in relationships,
upon reflection.

that's what we came here to do

whatever happens i pray that you choose the path
in confronting your demons. healing your past. looking at
your darkness. cultivating self-awareness and do the work.

why?

so that you stop unconsciously projecting your pain onto
other people and quite simply –

that's what we came here to do!

warm it up

so yellow
so orange.
so pink and brown.
our world is turning
so upside down.
and shining through
a new earth waits for you,
to put both feet forwards
and step into.

co-creating with the creator

what if i told you that god —
is actually a state of being.
of recognition.
of remembering.
a sort of gateway to the 'source'
and a code word into embodying that...?

oh how i want to know

crystalline, diamond, gold.
just harnessing my frequency yo.
tell me about staying stable in your frequency
no matter what is happening to you externally.
and how you transmute the energy
to stand unwaveringly.
in yourself.
in your power.
in your crystalline, diamond gold.
oh how i want to know...

welcome to 2020 / good morning my love

welcome to 2020
the year that everything shifted
in the direction that you chose
welcome to 2020
the time when you had all of the time
in the world to do whatever you've always wanted to do.
2020.
the time when the globe was shut down
because nobody really knew how
to control a virus
the fragility of the human experience
but
something didn't feel right
the figures lack context and
it's so hard to see the truth
when you can't actually see it
but
we stay inside.
going outside only
for food and walks in nature
and tell me...
what do you do when you stay inside?
how do you occupy your time?
how do you occupy your mind?
because those things you've been trying
to sweep under the carpet
are bound to rise
to the surface and
well — how do you? what do you?
welcome, to 2020
the time now.
where you decide
in 2020
you will decide

whether to open yourself up to your humanness,
to open yourself up to a whole new world
when you take that one step in confronting your shadow.
or whether you will close your eyes
and keep what's under the carpet under the carpet.
in 2020
it will be a pivotal moment in your life
if you choose the path into the deepest parts of your
mind, body, emotions, and your soul.
2020 it's a big one.
the red pill
or the blue pill
the metaphors become real
because they are messages
portrayed through storytelling
to help us to understand the deal.
take a closer look
at yourself
and then you will be able to
take a closer look at this world that we live in.
things will start to become clear.
we are and have been run
by darkness
the darkness of virtue-less leaders
who just contribute to this old soul destroying system,
the matrix,
take the red pill
or the blue pill babe
it's your choice
but
welcome to 2020,
the year when the veil is lifted
and we can no longer let the darkness run the show
because it has been brought to the the light for a reason,
and that reason
is in order for us to confront it.
collectively we see

individually we act.
the darkness is in us all.
2020
it's time to confront it.
you, me, her, they, he, we, she
now.
us.
welcome to 2020.
the year of the great awakening
and evolution of consciousness.
i know what path i'm treading.
2020
a time to be excited.
because
it has only just begun.
good morning my love.

i write poems

i write poems to help me get out of sticky situations.
when the road is unclear.
when the colours aren't fully defined.
i write poems to clarify my mind.
journal and refine.
release what needs to be released
burn it up in the fire.
i write poems to reflect
what's already buried deep inside
to come to the surface and align.
i write poems to heal through rhyme
and i will be writing poems
until the end of time.

welcome to the mysteries

if you want to come and find me,
you can meet me in the mysteries.
you know.
in that place that is no place but has a space here on earth.
most of my time is spent here.
between this dimension and that dimension.
through following my intuition.
relentlessly. until it all becomes clear.
i am lost and i am found.
floating between a boundless nature.
i am here.
in between paradox.
it's confusing, yet understanding it makes so much sense.
it's so clear.
because right here.
right here on this beautiful planet we call earth.
right here in this reality of waking and dreaming and day
dreaming life. right here.
the magic will appear.
if you can encompass everything and nothing and
everything in between that.
please. do not try to box me. for i am. for i am.
are you too?
then let's swim and dance in the grand, mystical journey
that lies within, amongst and before us.
as we travel through, to, in and out of.
welcome.
to the mysteries.

notes from my future self

i can't wait for you to see
the woman that i'm becoming.

phoenix rising

in the process of becoming
we let go of everything we thought,
aimed for and wanted ourselves to be.
to be humbly satisfied with who we are instead.
because outside of our beliefs,
what we will see;
is that *we are so much more*
than what we had *ever* dreamed.
it's time to fly
honey pie.

set you free

and then you will see.
that the very thing
that caused you so much pain,
is precisely
what is going to set you free.

i am magic wildfire rose tinted gold

i stand in the power of knowing who i am.
i stand in my sovereignty inside outside inside forever.
i stand in the expression of my femininity
and that is how i create it not how you want me to be.

i rise as a woman.
yes. i rise as a woman.
i rise as a woman in this world
which forbids true expression of her divinity.

i rise in my gentleness. softness. in my certainty.
in my subtle expression of sensitivity.
i know that emotions are powerful alchemy.
and embrace them all wholeheartedly.

i don't need you to tell me who i am
or who i should be.
trust me.
i'm not looking for anything outside of me.
this. here. now.
and i appreciate that you say
you can see points for my growth.
but honestly,
what you see is a mirror reflection of you
than anything else you know.

i don't need your words to validate my existence.
i am magic wildfire rose tinted gold.
and if you can't see that
excuse me,
while i continue to unfold.

breh yous been sleeping all day,
night and century yo. and
ain't that my problem though.

because i know
that my expression is enough.
i am whole.
this woman right here is enough.
and she is powerful.

divine feminine is rising
and her expression is this:
i stand in my power.
please don't try to morph me
as you see fit.

trust in the relationship with yourself

trust you.
i know you got this and you know you do too.
and you already know this but imma say it again –
everything that you're looking for
lies deep within.

you must create

on the adventure of absorbing and expressing art
we long for those moments to meet our compadres
when serendipity speaks us into collaboration
unduly embraced in another kind of imagination
that wants to pull through
beige tones a kind of blue
unknown ye that too
in the mist of being you
a whisper guides itself into expression
and paths are trailed into other kinds of impressions.
you must follow the call
in ways that reveal all
of your artistic manifestations
revealing that which lies deep
within the channels of creation.
you. must. create.

bun babylon

bun babylon.
let's get lost in the truth.

awaiting, our bloom

we are shifting the energies
and clearing our timelines.
all of our densities
from over the years,
all of our blockages,
our ancestors tears,
for new paradigms create,
abundant ideas.
we are starting again from a
zero-point field.
i said,
we are starting again
from a zero-point field.
i trust that i got this
and know you do too.
'cause a new earth is in view
awaiting
our bloom...

when you detox your body

when you detox your body
do you detox your mind?
do you detox the remnants
of stagnancies that you hold?
do you detox your thoughts?
and your limiting beliefs?
do you detox the stress that
lives within your being?
when you detox your body
do you detox your soul?
tell me, is your detox conscious
or is your detox unknown?

level up

the next chapter of your life is going to require you to___.
every single thing is an opportunity to___.
there is nothing else left to do but to___.
you can either sit in your ignorance or you can___.
the road is splitting in order for you to___.
you choose the path of liberation when you___.
the pain is just a blessing to show you how to___.
your healing begins as soon as you___.
and it is your decision whether or not you will___.
but the energy is ripe for you to___.
it is time now my dearest one to follow the path of truth and to___.
you will be received in glory once you do___.
we got you when you___.
do what you came here to do and

level up.

the purge is here

we learn our deepest lessons and we heal our deepest wounds.

the purge is here for us to see our shadows and to accept our hidden truths.

remember the route

and finally. the age came where they started to realise the truth and remember their route back to the emerald city.

unlocking key memories of a past long forgotten. hidden actually, and suppressed.

a technique used by the dark forces of the unconscious because they don't even remember and continue to chase false values. continue to chase the illusion.

but the truth exists right below your nose. and the biggest deceits are hidden in suppression and suppressing the truth.

anything that brings you into separation is just a mind control game. unity is the truth and we are making our way home.

are you ready my love, lego?

organic

i am here to activate and embody
the original human blueprint.

rise my warrior rise

rise my warrior, rise.
it's time to wake up from the slumber
of this world that enslaves and teaches the ways
of the false light.
stand in your power.
it's time to recognise the truth of who you really are.
within your softness is your strength.
your ego won't take you very far because
your sensitivity and vulnerability are required
for you to become stronger.
to stand in your light.
you are so much more
than what they'd have you believe.
your power lies in defying everything they taught
you about becoming a man.
you've got to let the untrue unbecome you.
it's time to step away from the distorted masculine
and step into the divine masculine.
to learn the ways of sacred touch
and sacred sexuality.
and find unity with your own feminine.
the truth of who you are awaits you.
and you will know the difference because your soul
is already calling.
don't let them tell you how to be,
a man.
your soul already knows what that truly means
and it will take a little something something to step
away from the brainwashing –
this is precisely your path.
to walk away form the darkness in unconsciousness
and to step into your light and shine.
for it is time
to rise, my warrior,
rise.

enter the light

enter the light.
light that banishes all dark forces.
all old systems of operating.
sends it back to the universe for healing.
light that feels safe.
light that is your home.
light that sees to the truth
and nothing but
the truth.
light that transmutes all low density programs
we are running that do not serve us.
enter,
the light.
light that speaks courage into our actions
so we can walk straight into our heaviness.
straight into our shadows.
light that leads us through and out of them into peace.
light that knows no bounds.
light that shatters those low vibrations and cycles
as soon as it enters our bodies.
light that helps us to reclaim our bodies.
our sovereignty.
our power,
in this body.
in this land.
on this planet.
yes please,
enter the light.
light as a feather kind of light.

the story

see the story.
feel the story.
let go of the story.
change the story.

hit me with that new new fresh view

when you truly look – that's when you start to see.
that our perception in this reality
is hidden to a deceptive way of being.
but the more you look
the more you will see,
that nothing's really quite ever
as it seems.

you know what to do

confusion is the program
fear is the game.
the war is on our consciousness
and the quest is opposite blame.

it is you

and in the end of it all.
it is up to you.
where you want to grow to.
do you create peace — or conflict?
do you reside in love — or fear?
do you search for clarity — or confusion?
nobody can help you to iron out the crinkles in your mind.
and in your body. but you.
nobody can help you experience more joy.
and listen. you have to go to the darkest part.
the dark night of the soul is what they call it.
you must go there. to experience it.
just so that you know.
and so that you can climb your way out of there.
and then bring the gifts of what you found there
to the world.
it. is. part. of the journey.
but you must move through it.
less self-loathing and more self-observing.
there are tools that can help you through.
and. you will become the hero of your journey.
when you take those footsteps
toward the depths of your universe.
it is you my love.
it is you.

Printed in Great Britain
by Amazon